# UNCLE GRANDPA™

CREATED BY
PETER BROWNGARDT

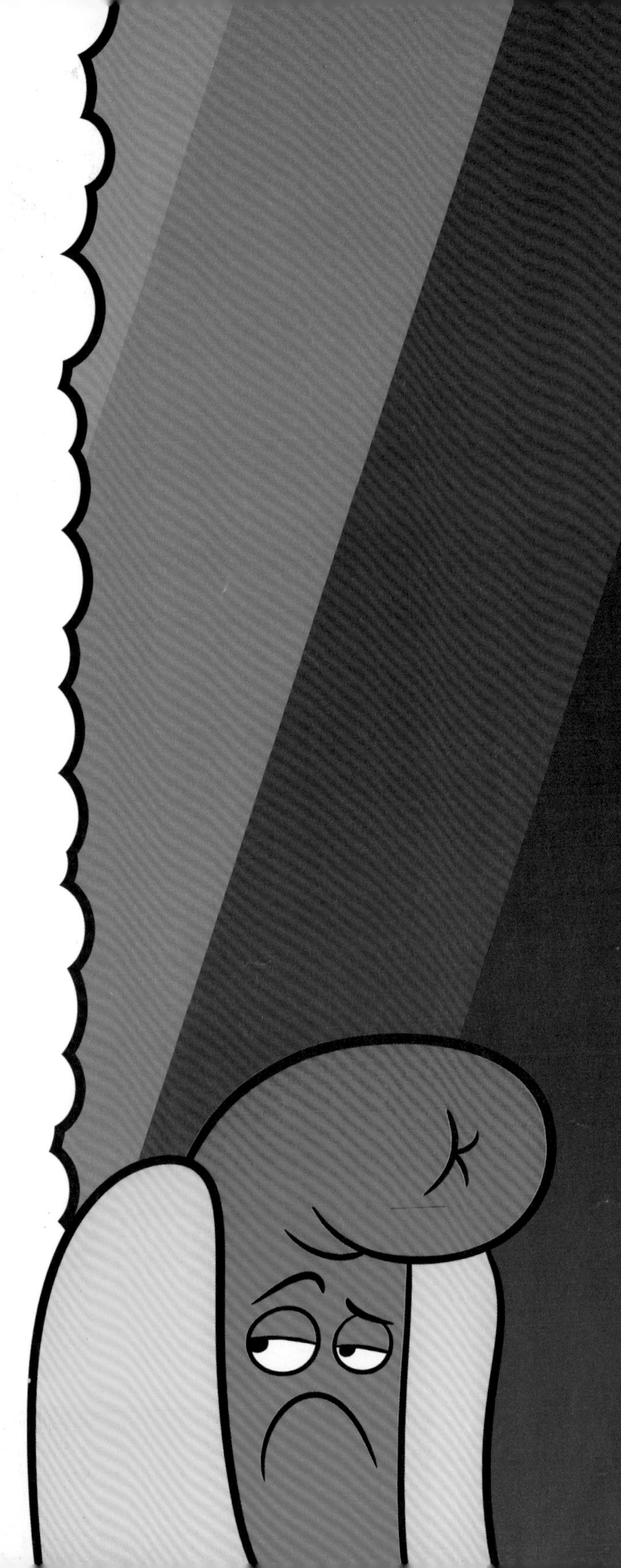

**UNCLE GRANDPA IN UNCLE GRANDPALAND, May 2017.**
Published by Titan Comics, a division of Titan Publishing Group Ltd. 
A CIP Catalog record of this book is available from the British Library.
Printed in China.
ISBN: 9781785861444

10 9 8 7 6 5 4 3 2 1

Written and Illustrated by
**PRANAS T. NAUJOKAITIS**

Colours by
**KAT EFIRD**
**E. JACKSON**
**ELEONORA BRUNI**
**MATTIA DI MEO**

Letters by
**TAYLOR ESPOSITO**

Cover by
**AARON ALEXOVICH**

With Special Thanks to Marisa Marionakis, Janet No, Curtis Lelash, Conrad Montgomery, Meghan Bradley, Rossitza Lazarova and the wonderful folks at Cartoon Network.

AT AN UNDISCLOSED LOCATION ON AN ISLAND IN THE MIDDLE OF NOWHERE...
Easy! Easy does it!
WARNING 10000 VOLTS
Easy! Don't want to damage the goods, do we?

UP
THUNK

And be careful! You don't want to lose an arm or leg yourself either!

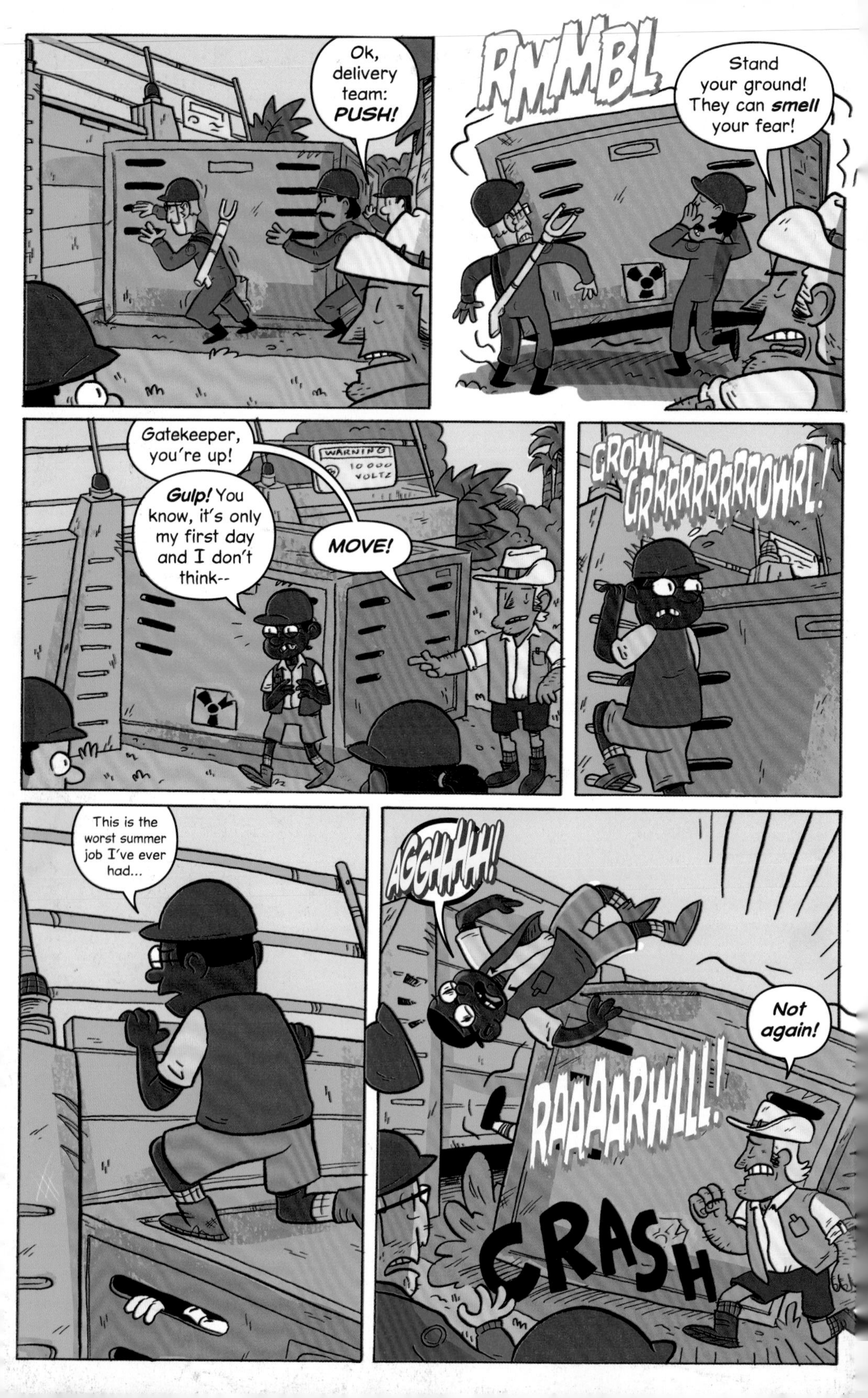
Ok, delivery team: PUSH!
RMMBL
Stand your ground! They can smell your fear!
Gatekeeper, you're up!
WARNING 10 000 VOLTZ
Gulp! You know, it's only my first day and I don't think--
MOVE!
GROW! GRRRRRRRRROWRL!
This is the worst summer job I've ever had...
AGGHHHH!
Not again!
RAAARHLLL!
CRASH

AGHHHH!
Help!
NOOOOO!
AGHHHH!
ZZZAP
ZAP
ZAP
ZZZAP
ZAP
ZAP
Stun him!
STUN HIM!
Ha... hahahaha! It's...it's tickling me!
HAHAHA!
HELP ME!
ZZZAPP
ZAP
ZAP
AGGHAHAHAHA, it won't stop! I'm dying!
HAHAHA!
ZZZZAP
ZAP
STUN HIIIIM!
ROOOOOOHLLLLOLOLOL!!
STUUUUUN HIIIIIM!
NOOOOOOOOOOOOOOO...
ZZZZZZZZZZZAP
STUUUUUN! HIIMMM!
ZZZZZZZZZZZZAP

CRASH!
Aw maaaaan! Not again!
Mom is gonna kill us!
Us? You're the one who threw the ball.
What?! YOU'RE the one who hit the ball that broke that vase!
Nuh-uh!
Uh-HUH!
Nuh-UH times infinity!
Nuh-UH times infinity PLUS one!
CRASH!
UG-RV

What? Koff!
Koff koff! Okay, NOW mom is gonna kill us!
GOOD MORNING!
Gasp!
UNCLE GRANDPA!
You know it!

So, what seems to be the problem here, kiddos?
We, were, uh, playing ball in the house and, uh...
Yeah, um, we, uh...
Say no more! We've all been there! Scientists have proven that playing ball inside the house is 53% more fun than playing outside.
SCIENTIFIC FACT!
Man, this vase is pretty broken. Or is it vase?
I realize now that that joke only works when spoken aloud and not so much in the visual medium of comic books. Sorry, kids!
Uh... who are you talking to?
Oh, no one.
Ok, noodle arms, do no harm!

Et voila! Good as new!
Wow!
Thanks, Uncle Grandpa!
Welp, my job here is done!
And next time you kids wanna play ball in the house, use a softball! Or just get better at sports. Either or.
Adios, kids!
Bye! Thanks, Uncle Grandpa!
Hi, kids! I'm home!
AGGGHHHH!
WHAT DID YOU DO TO OUR HOUSE?!
But look, Mom!
Uncle Grandpa fixed your favorite vase!
UNCLE GRANDPAAAA!
FÜD

Yes sir, another satisfied customer! Now, who's next on the list? Oof, there's a LOT today!
Oh, little Bobby is next! Ha, that kid's got some problems, I tell you what!
Hey!
BONK
Watch the road, Uncle Grandpa!
Huff huff! Halt! Hold it! I need to talk to you!
Huh? Did you say something, Belly Bag?
I said watch the--
OH NO! MAMA AND BABY DUCKS!
X-ING
SKREEEEEEEECH!
After you, ma'am!
WHOMP!
Huh?
What was THAT?

Hello?
Oh no! NOT AGAIN!
UG
Fancy suit? Fancy shoes? Fancy haircut? Oh no, he's a fancy businessman! He'll sue me and I'll be ruined for sure!
If he's still alive that is...
That's pretty dark, Uncle Grandpa! Even for you!
POKE POKE
Hello there!
AGGHHH! UNDEAD VAMPIRE!
You'd be surprised how often I get that. Sad.
Ah, Mr. Grandpa! Just the man I was looking for!
AGHHH! The vampire knows my name!
Run, Uncle Grandpa!

No, I'm not a blood-sucking, un-dead vampire. I'm a BUSINESSMAN!
Is there really any difference?
WINK
BA-DUM-BISH!!
Billy! What have I told you about practicing your drums in the middle of the street? It's not safe, dude!
Sorry, Uncle Grandpa.
Yes, yes, social commentary and jokes aside, I would like to introduce myself...
Ooooh, nice letterpress!
GUY BIZMAN
GB
SUPER RICH & SUPER PROFESSIONAL BUSINESSMAN
'Guy Bizman'? Really?
Now...how would you like to see your name up in LIGHTS?
GASP! LITTLE OL' ME?!

Wait a second...my name is ***already*** in lights!
See? Right there!
UNCLE HOT DOUG'S HOT DOG STAND
That's... a giant hot dog with a mustache.
*Huh.* Well I'll be! Guess it's time for me to get new glasses.
See? I told you that wasn't you!
Uncle Grandpa, I want to put you on the ***MAP! Literally!*** Give you the fame and glory that your brand, and everything that goes with it, deserves!
My ***brand?***
I want to build an ***UNCLE GRANDPA THEMED THEME PARK!***
And all you have to do is sign your likeness and life-rights away. It's just that easy.
CONTRACT
*Eep!*

Eh...I dunno.
I'd rather focus my time and energy on helping all the kids of the world (and sometimes the occasional small animal). That's what the Uncle Grandpa 'brand' is all about! That and tacos.
Sorry, I haven't eaten lunch yet, so I'm starving.
But just think of how many MORE children you could help if you open a theme park that they can go all year long!
So go on. Sign on the dotted line. You know. For the kids.
Uuuhhh...
CONTRACT
SIGN HERE
Uh, why did I just get an intense feeling of impending doom?
Pfft, it's probably just gas, Mr. Gus. You know how you get.
HEY GUYS! GUESS WHO'S GONNA BE OPENING UP AN UNCLE GRANDPA THEME PARK?
SMACK!
Spoiler alert: It's ME!
SLAM

Wait, what?
Some random businessman ran into the back of the RV and instead of suing me, he made me an offer to build an Uncle Grandpa themed theme park so I signed on the dotted line!
Yeah, it was super weird! Even by our standards!
Yeah, sure. Why not?
Mreow.
Seems legit.
And you're all going to help!
Wait, what?
You know, Uncle G, I always wondered when you were gonna cash in on your brand. I would've done it myself, but you know, I just got too busy living this rock n' roll lifestyle of mine.
C'mon, guys! Let's get brainstorming to help design the bestest, most FUNNEST theme park EVER!

We need a main hub to mark the center of the park. Something that screams 'Uncle Grandpa'!
What if we broke each part of the park up by theme?
Rides. You need the sickest rides any park has ever seen!
And you totes need a Pizza Steve Land so all the cool kids have a place to chill!
Aw man, these ideas are all gold! Keep 'em coming! There are literally no bad ideas, guys!
You could have a parade going three or four times a day! That's always fun.
...nd a Pizza Steve Land!
Growl!
You're right, a jungle safari adventure type land! You can head that area up, Giant Realistic Flying Tiger!
How about those rides with the spinning teacups? Every park has something like that.
Good call! Gotta keep the classics!
Pizza! Steve! LAND!

PIZZA STEVE LAND!
STOMP
STOMP
STOMP
PIZZA STEVE LAAAAND
Sigh. Ok, we'll, uh, pencil in that idea, I guess...
Ha ha YES!

It's so beautiful...
Uh...why is there no Pizza Steve Land?!
SNIFF

My dear Uncle Grandpa...welcome...to UNCLE GRANDPA LAND!
Um, why build a theme park on a tiny island in the middle of the ocean? That seems pretty... inconvenient.
Well...
There was a park here a long while ago. There was some unpleasantness. They were pretty vague on the details when I bought it.
But bottom-line, WE got the island for super cheap. It was quite the steal.
What kind of unpleasantness?
Oh, nothing too bad.
WHOMP
Eep!
We've dealt with that problem, don't you worry. And nothing like it will ever happen again. Trust me.

And HERE is where we'll start to build the park! The most luxurious park the world has ever seen!
Well, here you are!
Oh wow, my very own shovel! Thank you! I never had one before.
You have a whole closet FULL of shovels back home!
For this ground breaking ceremony I'd like to thank all the little people who made this possible! Hmm, not a lot of press at this ground breaking.
A ground breaking cer...oh, no no NO! That shovel is for you guys to get to work and start building this park! We have a deadline to meet, people!
The contract you signed says that you and your friends have to help build the park. It'll help keep labor costs down.
CONTRACT
U.G.
Uncle Grandpa...did you not read that contract before signing it?
Um...I dunno? Not really?
But hey, no biggie, right? Besides, this'll be FUN! How many folks get to build a theme park?
Well, properly highly skilled and paid contractors and workers, for starters.
Details, details!

Hey, Mac! Did any of yous orders a theme park?
Yo!
Aw'right, this is da place! Set it downs here!
Oh boy!
THEME
Uh...
THEME PARK
PIECES: 42,706,314
AGE 16+
U-BÜLD
UP
THUD
OW!
Yeah, total piece of cake! Heh...
Groan...
If I had bones, this would be so much more painful!

Well, you all seem to have this under control. Now if you excuse me, I have some very important business matters to deal with...
So let's get this bad boy opened up...
No, *wait!*
WHOOOOOSHH
UG
Whoa, what a rush!
*Groan...*
You know, if you keep frowning like that, you're gonna get wrinkles.
UG

Aw nuts! All these instructions are in Swedish or some-thing! I can't build this!
pärk
Ugh.
Oh please, the whole "can't put together Swedish flat packed build-it-yourself furniture" gag is such a tired joke!
If you just follow the clearly pictured step-by-step instructions carefully...
You get a perfectly put together product! Anyone with even half a brain can do it.
Uh... guys?
Case in point...
Someone call the doctor... please...

Okay, just need to connect these few wires...
Pffft...
These kinds of rides are for babies! Give me some-thing with some SPEED!
You want SPEED, huh?
INSANE
NORMAL
Ha ha! NOW we're talking!
Uuuhhhh! No, I'm gonna hurl!
WAAAAAHHH!
AGGGHHHH!
STOP THE RIDE!
WE'RE GONNA BE SICK!
STOP
Uh oh...
Okay...maybe that was a little bit too fast.

I'm putting you in charge of blowing up all these balloons. There's no way you can get hurt doing this. Sound good?
Not getting hurt for the sake of a joke is a-okay by me, Mr. Gus!
BALLOONS
$8.00 EACH
PSSSSSSSSST
He
Hey, Giant Realistic Flying Tiger! Check it!
FFFFFFffff
Look at how funny my voice iiiiiiiiis!
Heh heh heh!
LATER...
Typical that Pizza Steve wouldn't finish filling these. Also, these are some really creepy looking balloons.
eep!
Hmmmm...

Alright, just gotta turn on the power and...
WILL UNCLE GRANDPA AND FRIENDS PLEASE REPORT TO THE MAIN PARK BUILDING!
My ears and brains!
Well, at least the intercoms now work...
HUH? WHAT? DID YOU SAY SOME-THING?
UG
Whoa!
Boy, I hope this all doesn't give me a BIG HEAD! Haw! Get it?
Wow, living large, Uncle G!
Uncle Grandpa, you're better than that!
Is he, though?

Ah, good! You made it!
I have a surprise for you.
Growl?
Aw girl, you're always thinking with your stomach!
Our park scientists *just* finished perfecting their latest innovation in park entertainment and service.
I give you...
ACTIVA
Our *army* of Uncle Grandpa *costumed mascots!*

These will populate the park, doing menial tasks. Ticket sales, running the rides, manual labor, all of it. They'll even help finish up building the park with you.
Woooow! It's like looking into a mirror! A HANDSOME mirror!
Wow, what poor suckers did you get to wear these things?
Oh. They're clones. Obviously.
WHAAAAT?!
Well, we crunched the numbers and it turns out it's actually cheaper to bioengineer an army of clones instead of hiring a bunch of suckers, er, I mean, college kids as interns over the summer. Also, less labor laws to deal with.
Pfft, no way! You're just pulling our legs. Let's yank this mask off and see who our "clone" really is!
YOINK
Eeeeeer! Goo'd-a mor-n'ing!
BZZZZ

AAAAAGGHHHHH
Yarp?
The cloning process didn't go *quite* as planned. There were a few...bugs. But they still function. For the most part.
But what about the moral implications of cloning? And the potential dangers? Life will find a way, and all that jazz?
Simple. We engineered the clones to obey *all* orders and modified any negative thoughts they may have through this very scientific and very expensive looking computer system.
And that said computer system controls the clones with these here microchips in their brains. Again, it's *ALL* very scientific. And 100% safe.
Duurrrr...
*What?!* That all just raises even *MORE* questions and concerns!

Also, where did you get a sample of Uncle Grandpa's DNA?
Mr. Gus! Don't be vulgar!
A FEW MONTHS AGO...
ZZZZZ
SNIP SNIP SNIP
ZZZ
WHAT?! That is HIGHLY unethical!
Huh. I wondered what happened to that side of my sweet 'stache.
Unfortunately DNA samples from mustaches are not 100% complete. We had some...gaps we had to fill in. So we filled it with the DNA of such animals as bears, sharks, alligators, and ill-mannered groundhogs. And also some cybernetics, to give them that real sci-fi cyborg feel, you know?
e=mc²
Hey, they may be freaky looking but these clones are alright by m-- WHOOOOA!
Uh, was this thing important?
Grrr-- ERROR! ERROR! 404 NOT FOUND!
DES BZZZ DESTROY!

DESTROY!
AGGHHHH!
Good morning!
Hey now! We must be more careful!
So the only thing that's keeping all these clones from going haywire is one lone electrical chord?!
I'll have someone tape it down to the groun It won't happen again. Believe me.
But... what if the power goes out or something?
Oh, nonsense! The odds of that happening are a billion to one! So no worries! Now Uncle Grandpa, come with me. I'll show you your new executive office!
Ooooh, sweet!
Now get back to work. Rome wasn't built in a day, but this park will be!
Morning...

Aw, c'mon, Mr. Gus! Just admit you can't lift it.
I... grunt...can... uhf...DO IT!
AGGGHHHH!
Huh?
Whoa!
Huh. Freakishly strong, ain't they?
Gooood... BZZ ...morning!
Yeah...

Wha...?
Hey! Clones! You only put in **half** the bolts needed to support this beam!
Pfffft!
Good 'nuff.
**Duct tape?!**
Eerp!
GRADE F
**Hey!** Get out of there!
They are cutting every corner they can!
**They spared every expense!**

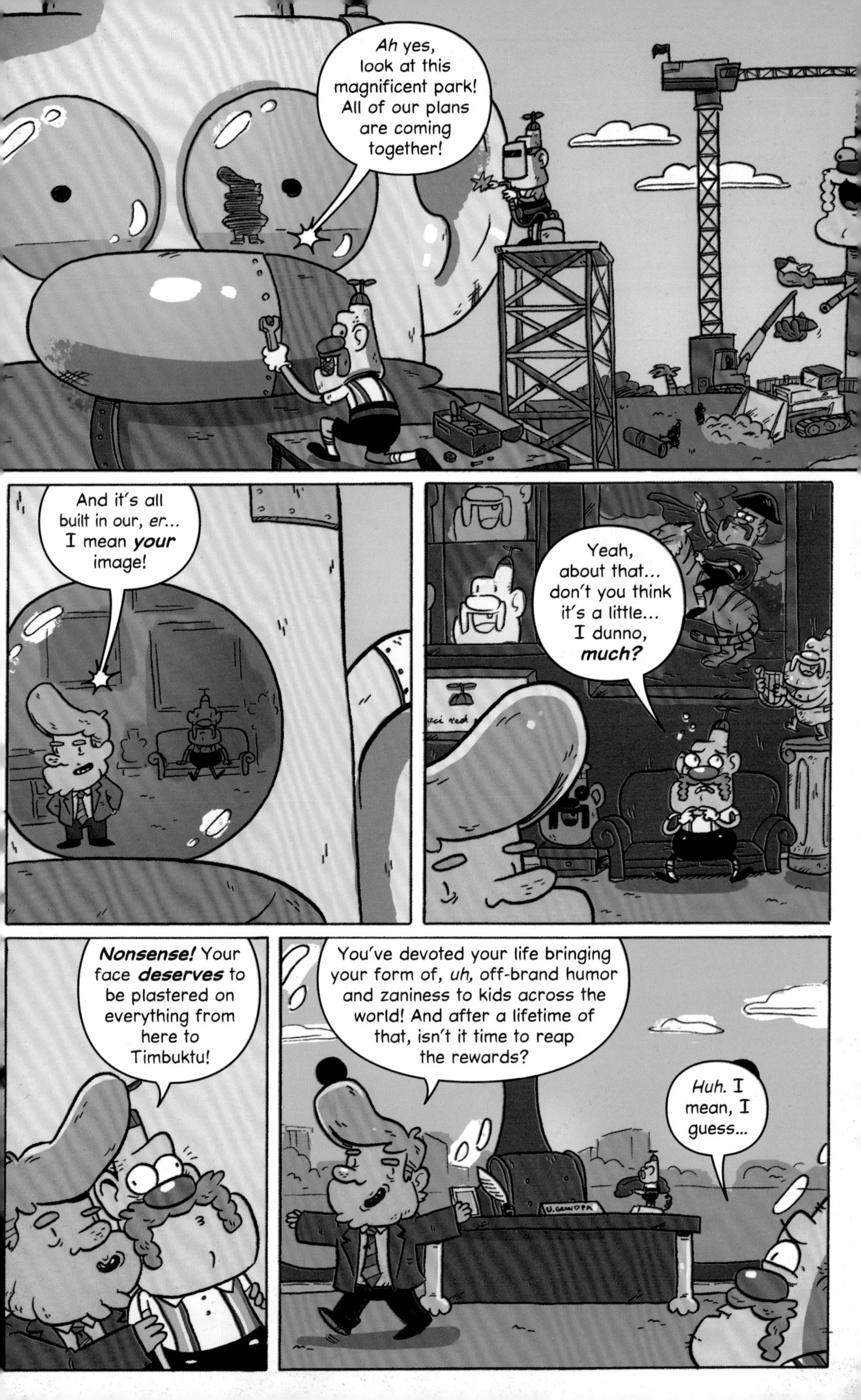
Ah yes, look at this magnificent park! All of our plans are coming together!
And it's all built in our, er... I mean your image!
Yeah, about that... don't you think it's a little... I dunno, much?
Nonsense! Your face deserves to be plastered on everything from here to Timbuktu!
You've devoted your life bringing your form of, uh, off-brand humor and zaniness to kids across the world! And after a lifetime of that, isn't it time to reap the rewards?
Huh. I mean, I guess...

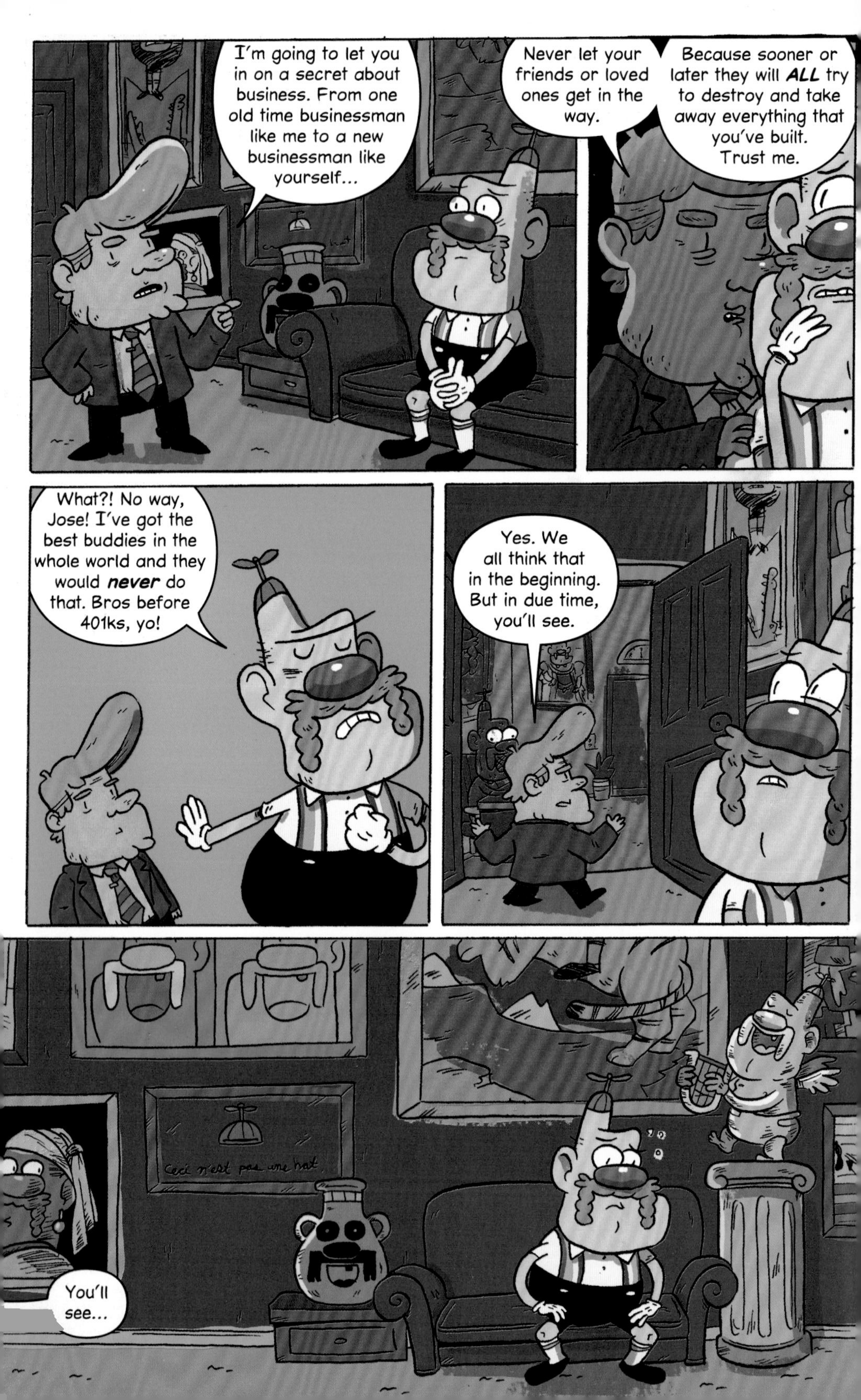
I'm going to let you in on a secret about business. From one old time businessman like me to a new businessman like yourself...
Never let your friends or loved ones get in the way.
Because sooner or later they will **ALL** try to destroy and take away everything that you've built. Trust me.
What?! No way, Jose! I've got the best buddies in the whole world and they would ***never*** do that. Bros before 401ks, yo!
Yes. We all think that in the beginning. But in due time, you'll see.
Ceci n'est pas une hat
You'll see...

Tsk tsk. Look at all this shoddy workmanship! Planks aren't even nailed down fully!
It looks fine to me, Mr. Gus.
WHOOOOOA!
HA HA HA HA HA HA HA HA HA HA
TRIP
SPLAT
RAAAAAAAAOWR!
Oh no! Giant Realistic Flying Tiger got a splinter from this unfinished and poorly cut wood!
Oh no, poor girl!
Whimper...
WHAT?!
So when I get hurt, it's funny? But when she gets hurt we all have to get sad? That's not fair, man!
Well, when you get hurt it's all slapsticky and cartoony. But when a realistic animal gets hurt, it gets serious.
Yeah, that's Storytelling 101 right there!
Mew...
Okay. Enough is enough! We gotta tell Uncle Grandpa about this!

Wow, this is all really coming together!
U. GRANDPA
Uncle Grandpa! We gotta talk!
No! No go in! Have appointment!
We don't need an appointment, pal! I'm a VIP! A very important pizza-man!
It's okay, Clone-85! My friends are always welcome! Come in, come in!
Daaaang, this is one fancy office, Uncle G!
Isn't this whole thing so cool, guys? I'm so glad we're doing this together! So, what can I do for ya, dudes?
U. GRANDPA
Uncle Grandpa... we gotta shut this park down.

'Scuse me, I didn't hear you right. Think I have some ear-wax in here.
Ah, there we go, much better! You were saying?
We gotta shut this park down! At least until we can make sure it's being built safely.
WHAT?!
I...I don't believe this! Bizman was RIGHT! My friends are trying to destroy my dreams!
Your dreams? You didn't even want to build a theme park until YESTERDAY! People are going to get HURT out there if we don't do something!
Maybe...maybe it's best if you guys all left my park.
Uncle Grandpa... what are you saying?
Just go! I can run this park myself!
But...
Mew?
GO!
U. GRANDPA
C'mon. Let's go. We're not wanted here anymore.
Mew...
Dang. That's ice cold, Uncle G!

Let's blow this popsicle stand!
But...but we can't just leave Uncle Grandpa!
He made his choice! He doesn't want us around anymore. And I don't want us to be here when this whole thing comes crashing down! Literally!
Now let's find the RV and get out of here.
Oh, hey guys!
I ♥ FUN
Check it out! I just finished turning the RV into a sweet new park ride! Pretty cool, huh?
UG
Great! Now we're stuck here!
THANKS a bunch, Tiny Miracle!
Yeah, way to go, you bucket of bolts!
Rarw!
I...sniff...I was just trying to help!

They are on the move, sir.
Hmm. They are the one loose string in this whole operation.
Should I detain them, sir?
No, I have a better idea to keep them... occupied.
Hey there! How goes it, friends?
What do you want?
I heard about the unfortunate falling out between you and Uncle Grandpa.
It's always such a shame when friends have a falling out. Sad. Truly sad.
ICE
I see your RV has been compromised and I can't afford to let one of our helicopters take you home until after the park opens.
But I do have an offer to help pass the time until then...

Mr. Gus, how would you like to be the head of park security?
What?!
This park is a disaster waiting to happen, why would I want to continue working at it?
And who better than you, someone who is so concerned with the safety of others, to help keep Uncle Grandpaland, and all of it's guests, safe?
I don't--um... huh.
AND you'd get a badge, a group of underpaid teenage workers to boss around, AND...
Your own personal transport vehicle!
I mean...I do hate walking everywhere.
Okay. I'll do it...but only to make sure everything is safe!
Of course!
Okay. Let's roll out!
One down...

PIZZA STEVE
LAND
You can open them now.
Say WHAAAAAAT?!
I wanted to wait until the park opened up to surprise you, but...
Oh man, this is SO cool!
But if it's not to your liking, we can just tear it down and--
What?! No way, man!
It's perfect.
And I'm never, EVER going to leave.
PIZZA STEVE
LAND
Very well, if you insist!
HA HA HA HA HA HA HA HA HA HA

Now I'd like you to taste test ALL the food we'll be serving here.
Whoa, wait...it's all you can eat?
Of course! Eat until you burst at the seams! Seriously.
HAPPY BIRTHDAY
I just can't say no to free food!
Oh, I know.
And I saved my most clever plan, er, I mean, job for you, Giant Realistic Flying Tiger!
JUNGLE SAFARI BURG
Mrow?
But how about dinner, first?
Mew? Purrrrrr!
ROOOOOOWRL!
SLAM
RAAAAAWWRR!
You really do think with your stomach, don't you?

And with them out of the way, now everything else can go smoothly.
Yes, sir.
Ah! Good.
RRRRRRIN-
RRRING
YIPES!
Hello? Uncle Grandpa here. How can I help you?
Good news! We just finished building the park and are ready to open!
Hot dog! That was fast!

Rachel Newswoman here, reporting live from the grand opening of Uncle Grandpaland!
PTN
RACHEL NEWSWOMAN
SLOW NEWS DAY FIELD REPORTER
Excitement is in the air as everyone gathers to try to be one of the first visitors to the park.
HEY! NO CUTTING!
At any moment the gates will open and we'll get our first look at this park that celebrates all things Uncle Grandpa!
Seriously, BACK OF THE LINE!
And what are you most looking forward too?
All the RIDES! I wanna ride until I PUKE!
I...I just want to meet Uncle Grandpa...
This just better be worth all the money I paid for this! QUIT IT!

PWOOF
NEWS
GOOOOOOOD MORNING!
Welcome boys and girls of ALL ages! You will all be the first to experience the most Uncle Grandpa-y place on Earth! A magical place that celebrates all the joy and fun that makes me Uncle Grandpa!
WELCOME TO UNCLE GRANDPALAND!

And as a way of saying thank you, I want to invite you ALL to come in for free today!
WOOOOOO!
ALRIGHT!
YEAH!
Ahem.
Uh...half-off admission?
Nope.
Free hat?
Not in the budget.
Free picture with me?
They have to pay for that.
How about a free high five?
Hmm... okay. I'll allow it.
Okay--
--FREE HIGH FIVES FOR EVERY-ONE!
Welcome!
Welcome!
Welcome!
SLAP SLAP SLAP
HOURS LATER...
Wel...come. Welcome...ow, not too hard, kid!
SLAP
Totally... ow...worth it...

ICE CREAM
UG
I ♥ UG
AR
Wow! This is amazing!
The guests are all having a great time!
Rides are running smoothly.
SPLASH ZONE
The air is filled with the laughter of children!
HAA HA HA HA HA HA HA HA HA HEE HA TEE HEE HA HA HEE HA
Yep. Just like the first day of any new theme park opening, everything is going *PERFECTLY!*

AGGHHH!
Aw, it's okay! Let your ol' Uncle Grandpa make everything right! It's what I do!
One Uncle Grandpa plush, please!
Eighty-five bucks.
But...this is MY park. Look, this is a plush of ME. See? Can't I just take one?
Sorry. Rules is rules.
Sigh Okay.
Here ya go! Good as new!
Eeeeee! Thanks, Uncle Grandpa!

Hey, wait a second! This is filled with old newspapers and un-hatched spider eggs!
Correction: HATCHED spider eggs.
Wha... these blades are ACTUAL blades! That's not safe!
HATS!
Run with scissors, kids! Drop out of school! Swim right after eating!
Hey, those are not good messages to be sending to the impressionable youth of the world!
This Pizza Steve toy is just a sack of flour! Who approved all of this shoddy merchandise?
Not only is that not mathematically possible, but I did NOT approve any of these!
110% U.G. APPROVED
Ok, clones! Get to approving!
Aaapprove
BZZZ
APPROVE!

Huh?
Loose bolts?
Where did you
come from, lil'
guys?
Huh?
KA-
BOOM!
MR. GUS'
CHURROS
Oh
geez!
Oh
geez oh
GEEZ!

Oh geez oh geez oh geez...
TAP
TAP
TAP
TAP
TAP
TAP
TAP
THUNK
What the...this load bearing wall is just painted over **graham crackers!**
OH GEEZ! WE SPARED EVERY EXPENSE!
**Hey!** You! What are you doing?
Huh?

Mr. Gus!
Oh... **hey,** Uncle Grandpa.
We were just checking out reports of a park guest destroying park walls.
*Oh, heh.* Well, nothing wrong with ***these*** walls, nosiree.
Everything in this park is running super smoothly and super safe, like I knew it would!
Well, call in a report if you see anything funny going on.
Okay. You got it.
Wait...when did Mr. Gus become a security guard here?
I must have missed that part of the plot. *Oh* well.

Hey, that's **MY** Pizza Steve toy!
Nuh **UH,** it's **MINE!**
HOT DO
Hey hey **HEY!** Friends shouldn't fight like this!
RRRRRRIPP
Now there you go! There's nothing I hate more than friends fighting!
Uh... thanks, Uncle Grandpa...
...I guess...
Yep. Friendship! **THAT'S** the ticket!
SLAM DUNK!
BEST FRIENDS
Oh man...
PINS $10
COOL.
That be $29.99. Pay.

Mr. Bizman, sir! It's... it's...
Spit it out!
We're tracking a hurricane, monsoon, typhoon, AND tsunami ALL headed for us! They are all going to hit us at the exact same time!
We've... we've never seen anything like it! EVER!
When they all hit, it's going to cut ALL power to the park! Even the backup power won't be able to take the hit! We're DOOMED!
Excellent. Everything is going according to plan.
Mwahaha!
EXI
Mwahaha!
Dude...is our boss evil?
Pfft, I dunno. Mondays though, right?

Is...is this what I really wanted?
I...I just wanted to bring more Uncle Grandpa-brand fun to the masses! *That's all!*
32
But at what cost?
Was it all worth it?
ST FRIENDS
BEST FRIENDS
*Uhhh...* This can't be good.

MAIN AVE
ARCADE
MR. GUS'
PAWN SHOP

CHARLIE BURGER
BURGERS

KABOOM
Oh no!
Oh no no no
no **NO!**
FZZZT
FZZZT
FZZZT
Good...
goood...
BZZZ
BZZZ
...gooooooo-
ooooooo...
BZZZ
BZZZ
...reboot...
BZZZ

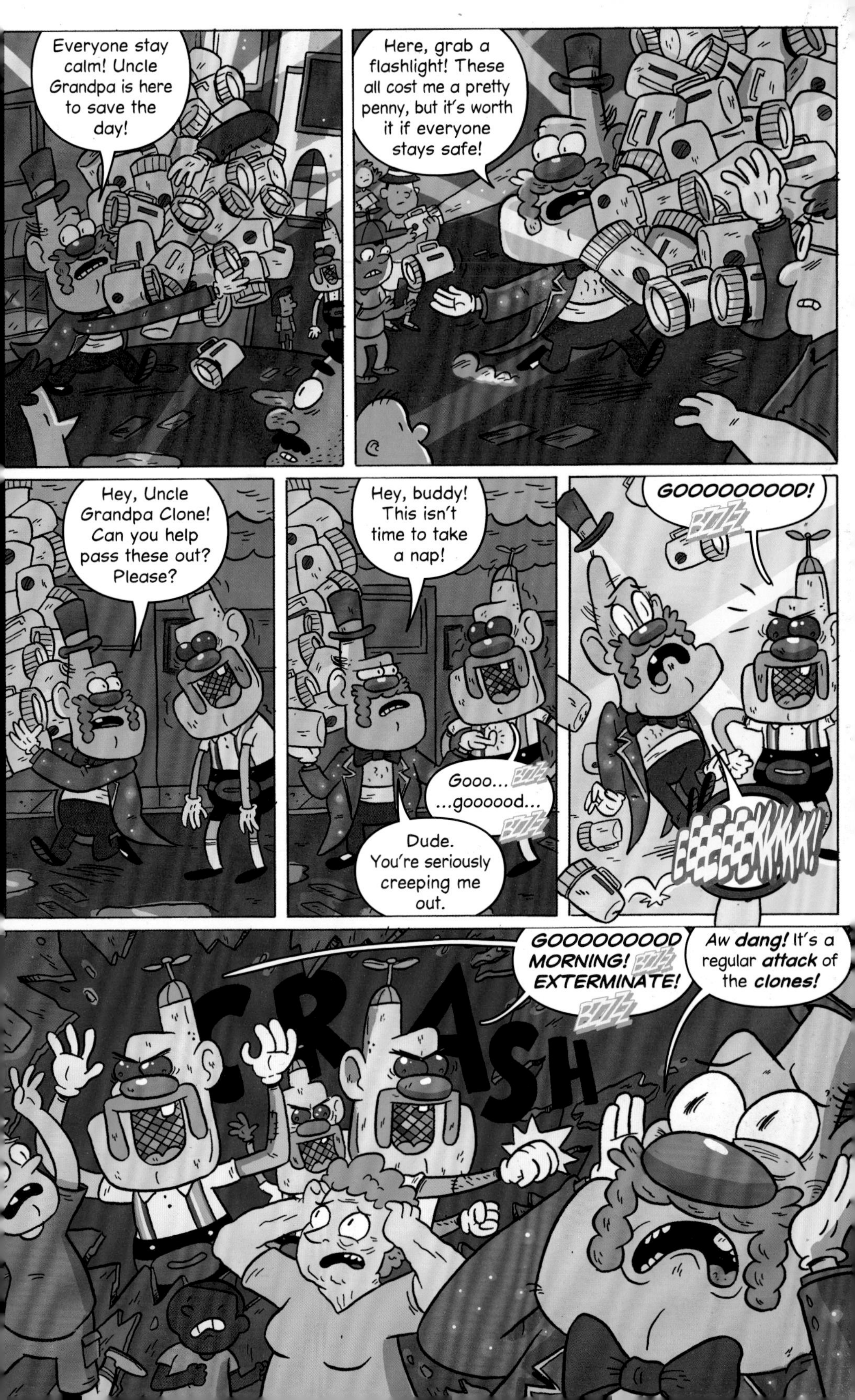
Everyone stay calm! Uncle Grandpa is here to save the day!
Here, grab a flashlight! These all cost me a pretty penny, but it's worth it if everyone stays safe!
Hey, Uncle Grandpa Clone! Can you help pass these out? Please?
Hey, buddy! This isn't time to take a nap!
Gooo... BZZZ ...goooood... BZZZ
Dude. You're seriously creeping me out.
GOOOOOOOOD! BZZZ
EEEEEEEKKKKK!
CRASH
GOOOOOOOOD MORNING! BZZZ EXTERMINATE! BZZZ
Aw dang! It's a regular attack of the clones!

Everyone please stay chill!
These clones are more afraid of you than you are of them!
Nope, I was thinking of bears! Yeah, everyone **PANIC!**
Don't worry, dear park guests! I'll save you ***all!***
You guys will be safe in here! I think.
MEN
***Oof!*** Sorry about the smell, kids! But ***hey,*** it beats getting torn apart by an angry clone army, right?
CLICK!
***Please*** don't put this in your online reviews...*oh geez...*

TOYS
Oh geez...

CRASH

CRUNCH

This is **bad!** This is really, really, ***really*** ***bad!*** I can't fix ***this*** on my own!

Ok. Time to round up the ol' team!

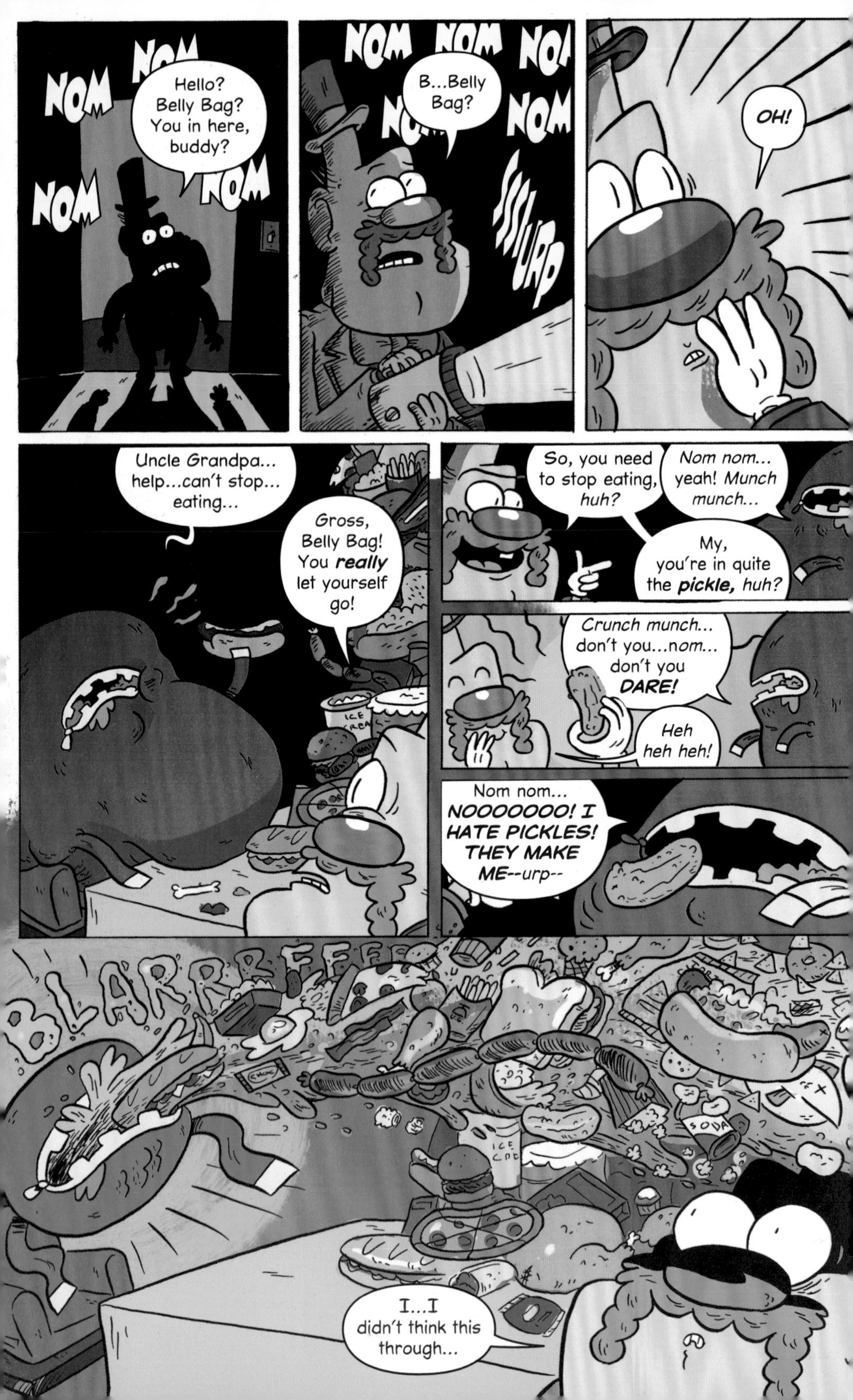
NOM
NOM
Hello? Belly Bag? You in here, buddy?
NOM
NOM
NOM NOM NO
B...Belly Bag?
NOM
SSLURP
OH!
Uncle Grandpa... help...can't stop... eating...
Gross, Belly Bag! You **really** let yourself go!
So, you need to stop eating, huh?
Nom nom... yeah! Munch munch...
My, you're in quite the **pickle,** huh?
Crunch munch... don't you...nom... don't you **DARE!**
Heh heh heh!
Nom nom... **NOOOOOOO! I HATE PICKLES! THEY MAKE ME**--urp--
BLARRRFFFF
SODA
I...I didn't think this through...

Wow, thanks, Uncle Grandpa! I don't feel like eating ever again!
Yeah... me too...
So why are you here? I thought you were too busy running your park?
So **everything** in the park is going **wrong! Nothing** works, **all** the merch is overpriced and shoddy, and everything is **falling apart! ALSO** four storms simultaneously hit the park at once, knocking out all of the power to the island, including the machine that was keeping all the clones in check! So now on top of all of this the clones are running amok and causing chaos! So I'm rounding up the old team to help save all the guests from certain doom!
Also...I wanted to say sorry for being such a butthead.
*Aww,* I forgive ya, Uncle Grandpa! Now let's get to work!
Knew I could count on you, Belly Bag! But first... a costume change!
RRRRRRRRRIIIIPPP
Uncle Grandpa, **no!** Hide your **shame!**
*Heh heh.* **Oops!** Thought I had my normal clothes on underneath!
Don't worry, I got you **covered!**

Alrighty, next we gotta get Pizza Steve!
KING PIZZA STEVE LAND
Be careful! I heard rumors that he's gone CRAZY!
Geez, this is like a maze! We might never find him!
Also, I never approved a Pizza Steve Land!
What's the matter, Uncle G? Jealous that MY park is better than yours?
Pi...Pizza Steve? Is that you?
C'mon, pal! Where are you?
PIZZA STEVE!
Oh, HEY guys! Welcome to the best theme park EVERRR!
Uh... what's with the small army of rats?
Like them? They were hiding in the dry wall when I got here. I'm basically their king now. No biggie.

Ahem! You know it's customary to kneel before a king, right?
SNAP!
HEY! Watch it, you dirty rat!
I take showers daily, thank you very much!
Geez! I think having his own little theme park has really inflated Pizza Steve's ego!
Said the pot to the kettle!
Hey, I wasn't this bad! Right?
So tell me, Uncle G, what brings you to my kingdom?
Well, uh...
DEEP BREATH IN
So everything in the park is going wrong! Nothing works, all the merch is overpriced and shoddy, and everything is falling apart! ALSO four storms simultaneously hit the park at once, knocking out all of the power to the island, including the machine that was keeping all the clones in check! So now on top of all of this the clones are running amok and causing chaos! So I'm rounding up the old team to help save all the guests from certain doom!
Is...is he passed out?
Hey, man, you try doing that much exposition in one breath!
Fair.

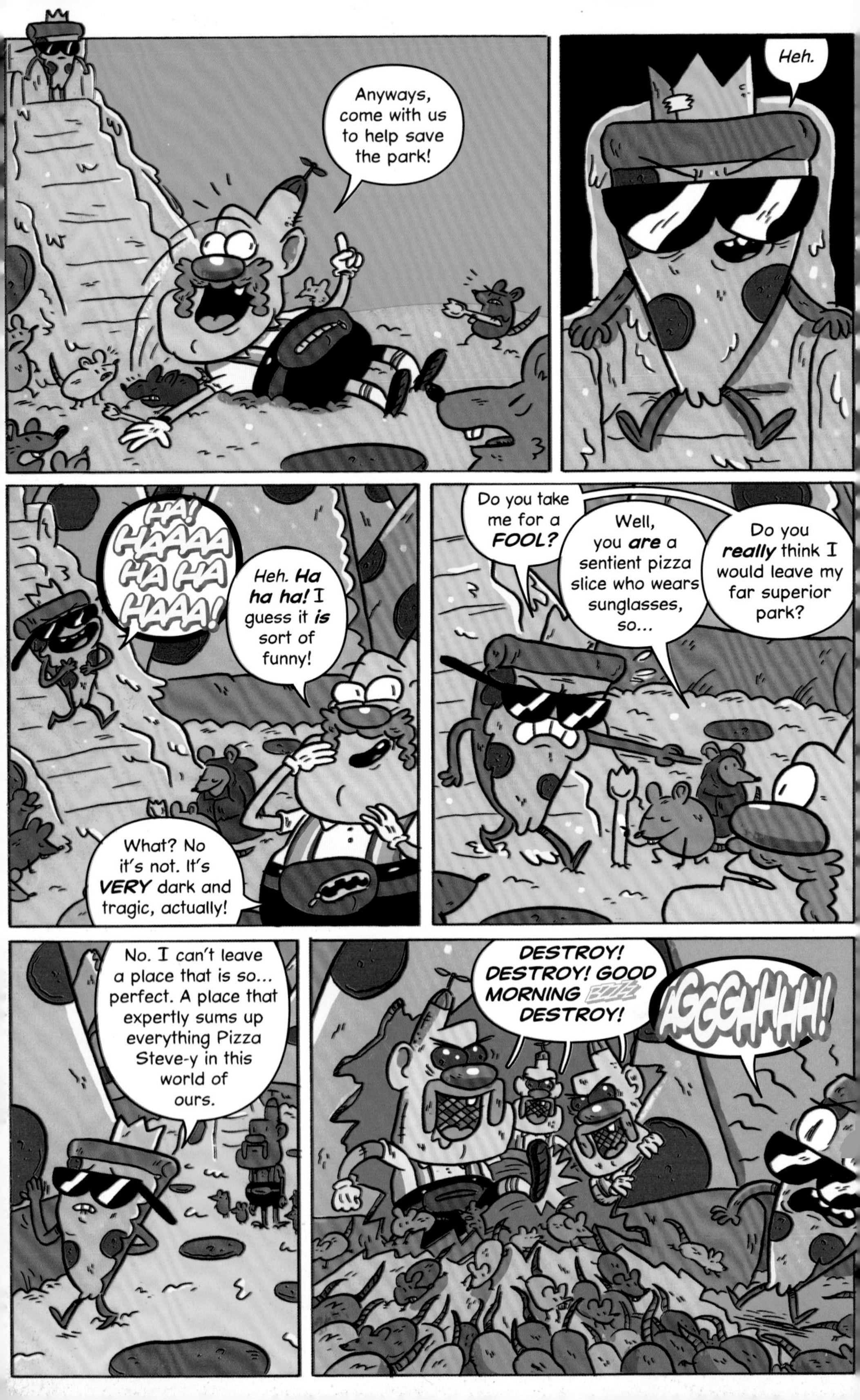

Anyways, come with us to help save the park!
Heh.
HA! HAAAA HA HA HAAA!
Heh. Ha ha ha! I guess it is sort of funny!
What? No it's not. It's VERY dark and tragic, actually!
Do you take me for a FOOL?
Well, you are a sentient pizza slice who wears sunglasses, so...
Do you really think I would leave my far superior park?
No. I can't leave a place that is so... perfect. A place that expertly sums up everything Pizza Steve-y in this world of ours.
DESTROY! DESTROY! GOOD MORNING BZZZ DESTROY!
AGGGHHHH!

My army! Defend your pizza king!
COWARDS!
No no NOOOOO! PIZZA STEVE LAND
NOOOOOO!
You monsters! You blew it up! You blew it all up!
STEVE
LND
Okay, Uncle G. I'm in.
Oh boy! Thanks, Pizza Steve!
You'll pay for this, you clones! YOU'LL ALL PAY FOR THIS!

Okay, let's hightail it outta here! Speaking of tails...we gotta find Giant Realistic Flying Tiger! Anyone know where we can find her?
Yeah, I heard some rumors...some dark, dark rumors...
Welcome one and all!
To the Realistic Animal Jungle Safari Show!
GROWL!
Now dance, tiger! DANCE!
Mrow...
KRACK
Ugh, this is so stuuuupid! Why do we have to watch this?
Hey, with how much we paid for this trip, I'm going to get my moneys worth!
Aww, poor Giant Realistic Flying Tiger!
This is so messed up!
Heh! It's kinda funny!
I got a plan... pst pst pst...

And now for our next stupid trick...
Woo hoooo!
Huh?
Everyone look at me, the mighty North American Uncle Grandpa Bear!
Wait, is this a new part of the show? Corporate didn't tell me about this...
Yep, everyone look at me and not at any of the other animals on the stage!
Especially not that giant realistic looking tiger over there, who I assume can also fly!
Uhh...
Psst! We're here to free you!
Um, duh! I think she knows that!
Mrowl.
Rowrl!
What? No! We don't have time to free any of the other animals! We have to--
GRRRRRRRR...
Okay. You make a pretty good argument.

Everyone keep looking at me, yep yep yep! I'm a bear! Whoop whoop!
Okay, look, we have to move on with the show here...
Huh?
TAP TAP TAP
AGGGHHHH!
GRRRRRR!
Heh heh heh!
ROWRL!
Aw, it was nothing, girl.
Mew?
Why am I here? Well...
Save your breath, Uncle Grandpa! Here, just read this.
Ooh, how meta!
Mrowl!

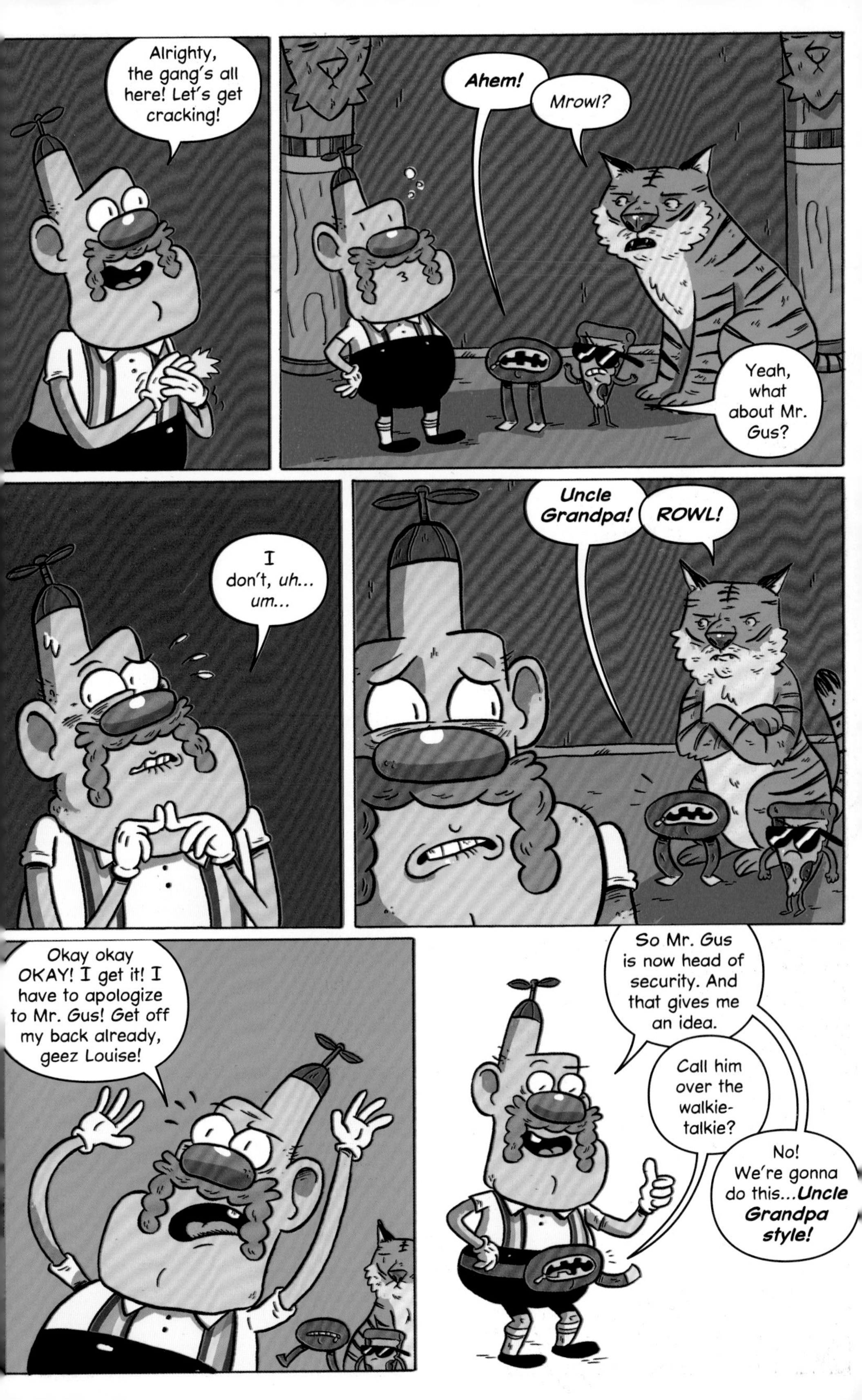
Alrighty, the gang's all here! Let's get cracking!
Ahem!
Mrowl?
Yeah, what about Mr. Gus?
I don't, uh... um...
Uncle Grandpa!
ROWL!
Okay okay OKAY! I get it! I have to apologize to Mr. Gus! Get off my back already, geez Louise!
So Mr. Gus is now head of security. And that gives me an idea.
Call him over the walkie-talkie?
No! We're gonna do this...Uncle Grandpa style!

Oh my, look at this loooong line for this side! Tee hee!
I guess I'll just CUT in front!
Heeeey, maaaaan! Back of the line, duuuuuuude!
Well shoot. That didn't work.
Heh heh heh...
KEEP OFF GRASS
Anything?
Nope.
Looks like I'm gonna have to take this...
TO THE NEXT LEVEL!
Hey! Those are prescription!

ALL EMPLOYEES MUST WASH HANDS
Ew, that's GROSS!
You know it!
NO
LOITERING
SKATEBOARDING
BEING SUPER RAD COOL
Wicked sick moves, girl!
Oops! I'm a regular ol' litter bug!
TOSS IT!
You know...
GASP!
If you wanted to get my attention so bad, you could have just called me on my walkie-talkie.
MR. GUS!

You know how many infractions I could write you up for?
Nine?
Oh it's all so terrible! You see what happened was...
Rides are spinning out of control. Storm knocked out all the power. Clones went crazy and are running amok.
Whoa, how did you know all that?
It's pretty easy to figure out what happened if you just look around.
Oh yeah.
Yeah, we've been trying to put out these fires for the past few hours. Like, literal fires.
I burnt my hand, man!
So what do you want?
I... uh...
I'm sorry, Mr. Gus! I was being such a butt-head, so self-absorbed in trying to get my fame and glory!

I now realize that the most important thing in life...is friendship. I'm sorry.
Oh Uncle Grandpa. I can never stay mad at you, you ol' goofball.
You're crushing all my internal organs but it's totally worth it.
TEAM UNCLE GRANDPA UNITE!
You two, patrol the park and do your best to get as many guests as possible to safety! I'll go with these guys and try to get these clones under control.
Yes sir!
Ok, gang! Let's save the park!

SALOON
1980s POST OFFICE
HALL OF ROBOTIC WORLD LEADERS
This is the *perfect* hiding *spot!*
Welcome to the *Hall* of *Robotic World Leaders!*
I'm confused. Does that mean they're robots *of* world leaders or world leaders of the robot world?
The only time anyone comes to these educational rides is to escape the heat, but since the power is out and there's no AC...
Man, these robots are creeping me out! It's a regular uncanny valley in here!
Mrow.
Ok, so let's formulate a plan here...

I've got my security team rounding up all the guests. What we gotta do is get to the building at the center of the park.
Word.
Once there we can manually restart the device that controls the clones to get them all under control again.
TAP TAP
Word.
Sounds easy **enough!**
Yeah. Easy except for the army of evil clones and broken rides that are standing in our way!
Word?
Oh yeah...
We could fly on you and get there easily.
mrow...
*Aww,* she can't because all this stress is blocking her up. It's okay, girl. Happens to the best of us.
Okay, that complicates things. Well...what I think we should do then is...
WHIIRRRRR...
WHIIRRRRR...
**Uh...** guys?
If you say ***'word'*** one more time I swear...

I cannot tell a lie...
I AM GOING TO CHOP YOU UP TO BITS!
Aw man, that's SO uncool, Mr. Washington!
Well, at least the backup power is starting to kick in, I guess.
There must be some-thing faulty with their wiring!
Alright, let's go, tough guy!
Pizza! Pizza!
First evil clones and now evil robots?
This is taking a really unexpected turn in the narrative!

Eat on
this knuckle
sandwich!
KLANG
Oh yeah...
they're made
of metal...
ow...
This can't
be how Pizza
Steve goes
out! By being
eaten!
RAWWWRRR!
Bully for
you!
Objective: Chop
down cherry
tree!
Hey, I
take offense to
that! I'm more
of a water balloon
with arms and
legs.
Well,
it's been nice
knowing you,
guys!
POW
Robo-Abe
Lincoln?
Four
score and
seven fists
ago...
Whoa! He
knocked his
block off!

Wait, why are you helping us, Robo-Abe Lincoln?
Flesh or robot, Abe Lincoln **always** fights for the side of honor and justice!
Now get out of here, you fools! I can't hold them off forever!
EXIT
We'll always remember your sacrifice, Robo-Abe Lincoln! If we survive this, we'll build a monument in your honor!

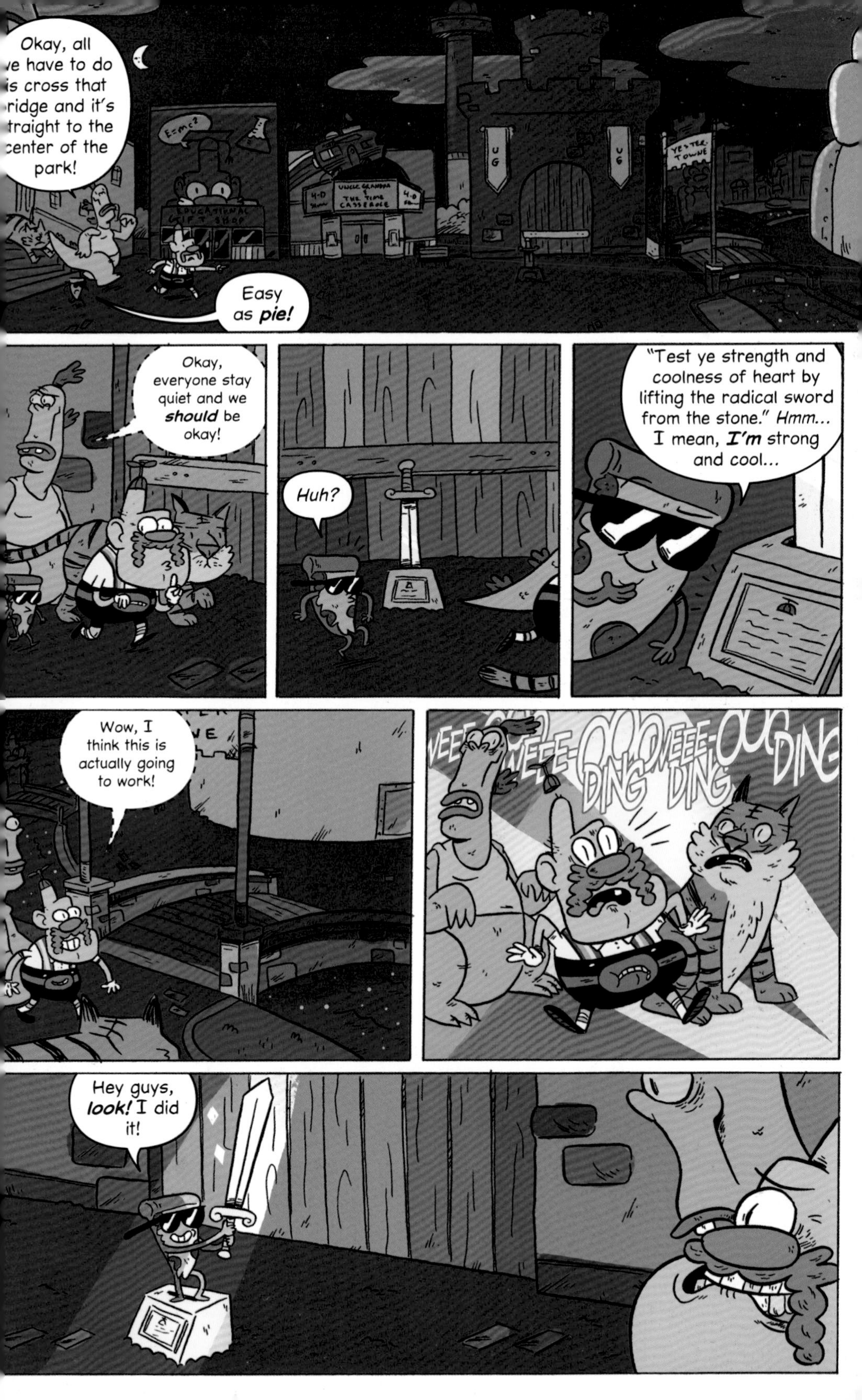

Okay, all ve have to do is cross that ridge and it's traight to the center of the park!
EDUCATIONAL GIFT SHOP
UNCLE GRANDPA & THE TIME CASSEROLE
4-D
UG
UG
YESTER-TOWNE
Easy as **pie!**
Okay, everyone stay quiet and we **should** be okay!
Huh?
"Test ye strength and coolness of heart by lifting the radical sword from the stone." *Hmm...* I mean, ***I'm*** strong and cool...
Wow, I think this is actually going to work!
WEEE-OOO WEEE-OOO WEEE-OOO
DING DING DING
Hey guys, **look!** I did it!

PIZZA STEVE!
Oh yeah...oops. Sorry, guys.
Hey! What that?!
Investigate! Investigate!
Well great! Now we have to take the long way around!
I said sorry!
C'mon. Let's move out.
Grrrrrrrr!
What do you mean I can't ride on your back? What, because of that? C'mon, I'm tiiiiiired!
GROWL!
Whatever. You guys are just jealous of my sweet, sweet sword.

Destroy!
Destroy!
Aw geez, I think they're getting closer!
We can cut through here. I think. Should also keep us hidden.
FUN" HOUSE
What the...heh. Hahaha!
Mew?
I think mine is broken...because this is how I look every day! Oooooh!
Ha ha! Man, these are some silly mirrors.
Hey guys, look at mine! I look just like a clone! Hyuck hyuck!
ACK! Guys...I don't think mine is a mirror!
Why are we always RUNNING?

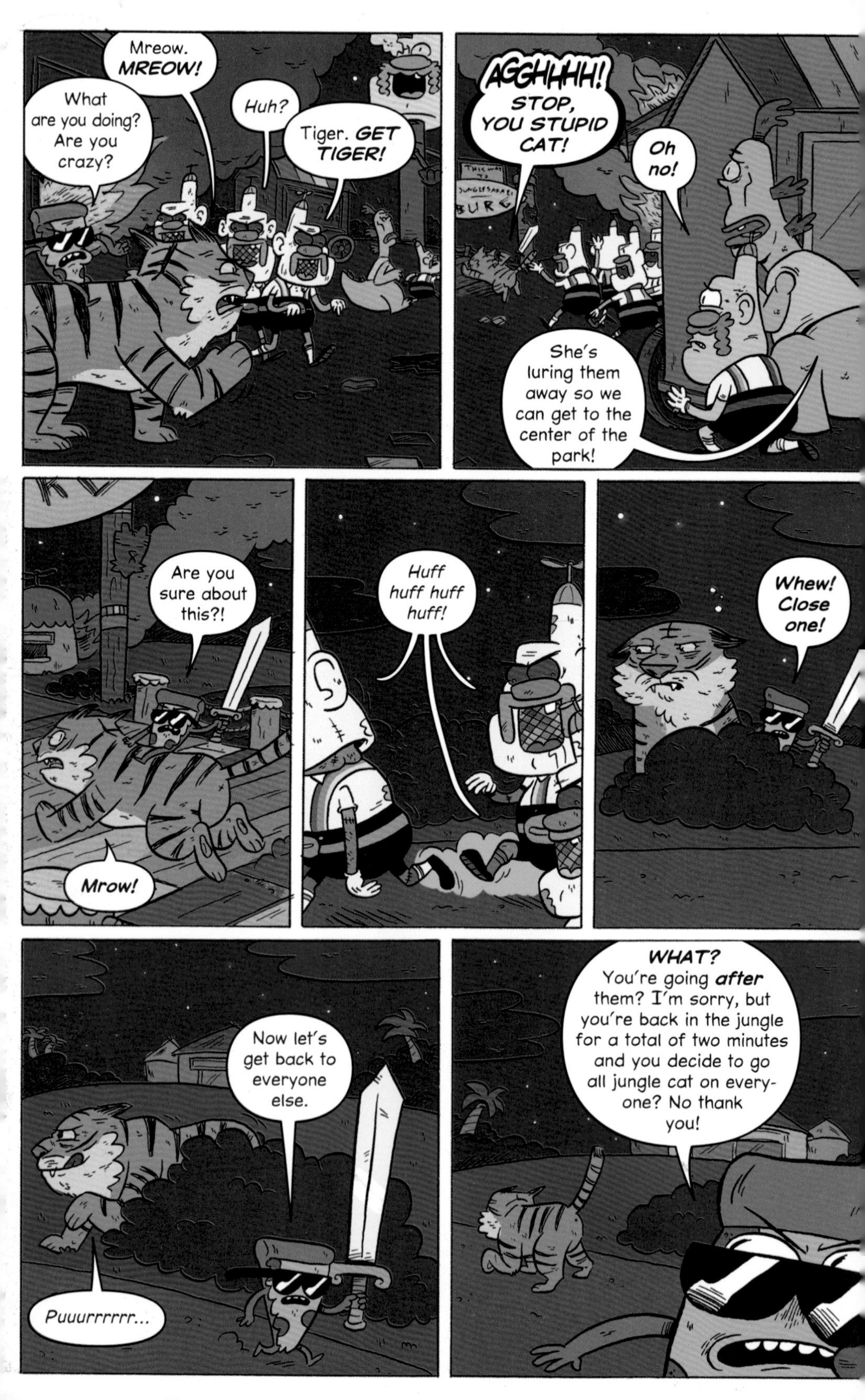

What are you doing? Are you crazy?
Mreow. MREOW!
Huh?
Tiger. GET TIGER!
AGGHHHH! STOP, YOU STUPID CAT!
Oh no!
She's luring them away so we can get to the center of the park!
Are you sure about this?!
Mrow!
Huff huff huff huff!
Whew! Close one!
Now let's get back to everyone else.
Puuurrrrrr...
WHAT? You're going after them? I'm sorry, but you're back in the jungle for a total of two minutes and you decide to go all jungle cat on every-one? No thank you!

You want to go all hunter, you can do it by yourself!
Giant Realistic Flying Tiger? Hello?
Pfft. Whatever. I can get back on my own.
And I'll get there in *style!*
PADDLE BOATS
I'm a sea captain, paddlin' down the river, paddlin' down the riiiiiiiver--
What the...?
THUMP
AGGHHH!

Go... huff...away... huff huff... wheeze...
Stand back! I'm not afraid to use this!
KRUNCH
Okay, you asked for it!
Heh...well what do you know. It wasn't even made of real metal. Oh boy...
Clever girl.

Do you hear that? Sounds like a clone screaming in terror.
Your mind is probably just playing tricks on you.
It's getting too dicey out here!
We should get off the streets again.
FUNNEL CAKE
In here, guys!
SLAM
Whew, that was a close one!
Oh no... it's about to get worse. A LOT worse.
We're all one happy world faaaaamily! We're all one happy world faaaamily!
We entered the We're All One Happy World Family ride!
We're all one happy world faaaaamily! We're all one happy world faaaamily!

We're all one happy world faaaaamily! We're all one happy world faaaamily!
Oh really, it's not THAT bad!
Ugh, my ears! Why did we even build this ride?
It really IS the worst.
I'd be more worried about the water we're standing in. Is that even water?
Help! Help us! Is anyone there?
Park guests! We gotta help them!
Don't worry! Uncle Grandpa is coming!
Hey, watch it!
Hold on!
world faaaamily!
Some of it went in my mouth.

Hey, are you okay?
We're all one happy world faaaaamily! We're all one happy world faaaamily!
Yeah, we're just **peachy!** We were fine hiding in here when the power went out, but now it's back and we're stuck here while this song just plays over and over and over and over--
Well I'll have you all out of here in a--
**WAAAAAHHH!** Keep him away! **KEEP HIM AWAY!**
Uh...
I'm sorry, it's not **you.** It's just those clones of you that are terrorizing the park...I mean, they look just like you.
Please... please don't take it personally.
Yeah...no worries...

So if you keep going that way, you'll get to safety.
Thanks!
Hey...you okay, Uncle Grandpa?
Sigh...
That kid was so afraid of me when I tried to help her.
Well...all the more reason to get these clones and this park under control.
Don't let it get to you buddy.
Here, how about you be in charge of the map.
Oh! Okay!
Oooooh, I know where we're gonna go next! Hee hee hee!
Ta-da! Dino-Bay! Don't you feel right at home now, Mr. Gus?
WELCOME TO DINO-BAY
Oh no...

Blech! What a horrible mish-mash of themes!
What's the matter, Mr. Gus? I thought you would dig this! Heh. Get it? Dig? Like bones?
Good one, Uncle Grandpa!
This is just...a total misrepresentation of dinosaurs! Of my people!
BIG ASTEROID BURGER
CAPT. RE
NOW SHOWIN
I mean, how would you feel if someone made a park misrepresenting you--?
Heh. Oh yeah...
Hey, no worries, buddy. This whole place is being burned down to the ground anyways.
Sigh... here we go again...
Yarr, exterminate!
Yarr, exterminate!
Yarr, exterminate!
Tsk. What a weak pun. Like, what does that even mean?
DINO-MITE RIV-ARR LOG RIDE
CAUTION!
ARR, WA YE STEP
Wait... why are we actually riding the ride?
ARR, WATCH YE STEP!
I'll be honest. I just wanted to sit down for a little bit.

Raaaarrr, me mateys! An' welcome to the story of Dino-Bay!
Oh joy...
Ah, a nice relaxing sit down.
Yo ho ho, rar rar rar! We be dinos of the seven seas!
Uh, I hope it's not TOO slow!
Walk the plank yaaar!
Raaaar, where be my treasure of buried bones, ya scalawag?
Aw, shut up!
AGH! Dang clones! Can't you give it a rest?
Uhhh...Mr. Gus?
Yar, prepare to be boarded!
I'm a little busy back here!
But... but...
Yar!
Why does the water just end up there?
You don't know how this ride ends?
HAVE A NICE DROP

Yaar!
AGHH! A drop?!
Yaaar BZZZ I've got scurvy!
Yeah! Oof! That's how log rides usually end!
We're sea captains, paddlin' down the river, paddlin' down the riiiiiiver--
MROOOOWL MROWLLLLLLL!
You know, after that crazy cool ninja attack you did back there, I've been enjoying this peaceful and uneventful ride down the river with you.
Mew.
AGGGGGGHHHHHHH!
Do you hear screaming coming from above?
Mrow.
AGGGHHHHHHHH!
OH NO!
GROWL!
AGGGGHHHHHHH!

Koff koff! Oh! Hey, guys! Mind if we drop in?
Could we cool it with the puns, please?
Groan!
You really know how to make a splash, huh, Uncle G?
Whew! These guys weigh a ton!
Phew, still alive. Just passed out.
PLOP!
Oh man, we're so close! I don't know how we're going to get past all the clones that I'm sure are now guarding it.
Hmm...
GOOD MORNING!
AGH! CLONE!
OOF! Hey! It's just me! Pizza Steve!
I...sniff...I just wanted to show you my cunning plan!
Oh geez, I'm sorry!
Hmm... you know he might be on to something here...

Good morning! Good morning! Good morning!
Dude, you're overdoing it!
What? You say 'Good morning' like fifty times a day! It's your catch-phrase!
Huh? I've never said that in my life!
Ha ha! I can't believe this is working! We're almost there!
Yipes!
Ahem!
Aw man, busted!
But... how did you know?
Puh-BZZZ-lease! We may be clone but we am not stupid!

Aw man! We got so close too!
Hello, Uncle Grandpa and friends!
Oh, hey, Mr. Bizman! Are we glad to see you!
Go inside and reactivate the clones' safety protocol! Hurry!
Hmm, yes, I could do that...
But I WON'T! That would just ruin all of my plans!
Wait, what?
Oh snap, is Mr. Bizman EVIL?
Honestly, we should have seen this coming from a mile away.

It's pretty amazing how easy it was to set up this trap for you. How easy it was to manipulate you. *All* of you.
*Oh* Mr. Bizman. Why you gotta be this way?
*Oh,* who? Guy Bizman? No, it wasn't ***HE*** who orchestrated this all...
It was ***I...***
NEGA-UNCLE GRANDPA!
GASP!

Wait, what? Who are you?
AGGGGHHHHH! YOU'RE ALWAYS DOING THIS!
Even since we were little kids!
Ooooh, I smell a flashback coming up!
"I was the neat and orderly one. Believing in structure. Doing everything by the book.
"And you, always so zany and chaotic! Always going off script!"
Goo-goo morning! Heh heh!
"And EVERYONE liked you more because of it!"
Awww, what a cute and silly baby you are!
Haw haw! Pbbbbbt!

"It continued through our teen years..."
Ahem, excuse me, Maggie? Would you do me the honor of accompanying me to the dance?
Umm...
Good morning!
Oh YES, Uncle Grandpa! I'll totally go to the dance with you!
Huh? What? OKAY!
ROTTEN TEETH
"And even into adulthood!"
So do I have the job, sir?
Actually...
We just filled the position. He's not qualified at all, but he sure does make us laugh!
HA! HA! HA! HA! HA!
Buy! Sell! BUY!
CAR WA$H
YOU! The screw-up! The goof-ball! The rule breaker! Were always getting ahead in the world! Always getting all the love and admiration! Everything handed to you on a silver platter! Nothing ever earned! And I've HAD IT! THIS ENDS NOW!
Huff huff huff...
I'm sorry, I zoned out. Who are you again?
AGGGGHHHHHH!
See what I mean?! He's always doing this!

No use losing my cool now. Not when I'm so close to finally finalizing my plan!
And what exactly *was* your plan?
Oh please. The villain spilling his guts in a monologue? What a trite trope!
But since I'm *NOT* the villain here, I'll tell you!
My plan was to build this park! A place that embodies everything Uncle Grandpa is and stands for! Truly the Uncle Granpa-iest place on Earth!
But the park would be rushed and shoddy, much like Uncle Grandpa himself. And the clones I created would go crazy when the four-part storm cut out the power.
Erp?
And all the guests here, sheep who were brainwashed into loving him, would experience pure terror with Uncle Grandpa's face plastered on it all! And then *THEY* would see Uncle Grandpa for what he truly is. A menace to society!
And then *you* would fade away from relevance and existence.
*Uh,* I'm still confuse about what going on her guys.

Yeah, except... um...
What?
There are a few, um, flaws with this plan of yours.
I planned. This out. PERFECTLY.
Yeah, that's the thing. It's overly complicated and elaborate and depends on every single thing happening perfectly.
Oh man, you're so right, Mr. Gus!
First you had to make clones. That had to be expensive. And not to mention a scientific breakthrough!
You could have used that science to, I don't know, cure diseases or something. Better mankind!
AND you had to get all that money for the cloning. And to buy the island, the rides, and the staff. That's a LOT of dough, man!
And what if Uncle Grandpa never signed over the rights to use his likeness for a park? Then this all would have been for naught!
Oooh, good point!
Mrow!
You're right, this ALL hinged on four storms hitting a small island in the middle of the ocean exactly on opening day! The odds of that are near impossible, yo! DO THE MATH!
RRRAAAGGHH

What part of well organized and thought out do you not understand? I planned a contingency for every contingency! And it doesn't matter anyways, because it all worked out the way I wanted it to, didn't it?
Sigh. See? This is how you and your kind are always getting under my skin!
But it doesn't matter anymore! I'm done. YOU'RE done.
Clones? Finish them.
SNAP!
Ooooooooh wait, I remember who that is! I think we met in the Army?
Shudder...

Ugh! We gotta get to that master clone switch!
C'mon, gang! Push! Put your weight into it!
Dude, I only weigh like four ounces!
I don't think we can make it...
AGGGHH! There's too many!
HISSSS!
Good night, everyone!
RRRUUMMBLE
Huh? Whuzzat?

My security patrol!
MROOOOWL!
My loyal rat subjects! Come, save your king!
And all the park guests!
Alright, everyone! Let's do this!

If just one of us could get up there, we can shut all the clones down.
Mrow!
You can fly me up there, Giant Realistic Flying Tiger?
You sure you're feeling up to it?
Mreow!
Okay, girl! Let's ride!
YEEEEEE-HAW!!

BZZZ
Err?
DELETE!
Incoming!
Mew?
HISSSSS!
ZZZZZZZZZZZ
OOF!
Got ya!
My hero!

You okay, girl?
Mrow...
Hey, don't worry! We'll find another way!
Okay. Throw me.
What? No way. You're so light you probably won't get even five feet in the air.
I'll go far if, and just follow me here...if you fold me up like a paper airplane.
But... that'll totally mess you up!
For real!
No! It's okay. This is my choice. And besides, I'm already kind of in the shape of a paper air-plane!
LET'S DO THIS!
OH! INSTANT REGRET!
No wait, I'm okay!
Nope, wait. No. Excruciating pain again!
WOOOOOOOO!
LET'S GO GO GO!
HA HAHA HA!

Oh dang, this just might work!
Fly, Pizza Steve! FLY!
AGGHH! Stupid hungry pigeon!
Well shoot...
Mr. Gus! If we can get closer, do you think you can toss ME up?
Wait...why don't you just use your crazy Uncle Grandpa powers to stretch up there or something?
Mr. Gus! You know full well I can only do that stuff when it's for comedic effect! And there is nothing comedic about our current situation!
Okay, okay. Yeah, we get closer I can toss you.
Alrighty, let's move it!
Me SMASH!
Oh wow. They left you in the oven a little bit too long, huh?

SMASH! SMASH!
SMASH
ME SMASH!
Hey, we GET it! We got a real broken record over here!
Ugh, it's no use! We gotta get closer!
SMASH!
Oh hey, I'm still alive!
SPLAT
PIZZA STEVE!
GAAAAAHHH!
Yeah, turns out that pigeon was a vegan. So you know, lucky me.
Okay, well...I'll be hanging out here if you need me.

You ready, Uncle Grandpa?
You know it, Mr. Gus!
Alley OOP!
CRASH
Belly Bag? Why am I in so much pain right now?
Probably the broken glass.
Oh yeah.
U-GR
Oh hey! The clone master switch thingy!
Boy, that was easy!
Sorry, clones but your days are, uh...shoot can't think of anything witty to say. Oh well!
JUST FLIP IT!

Oh! I know! Lights OUT, clones! HA!
AGH! Why isn't it working?
TAP TAP TAP TAP TAP TAP TAP TAP
Have you tried turning it on and off again?
Seriously. I put so much into planning this all. Did you really think I'd let my brilliant plan be foiled with a simple flip of a switch? Puh-lease!
CRASH
BONK
U. GRANDPA
Yep. More broken glass. Ow.
U. GRANDPA
Oh no...
HEY! Come back here and perish with everyone else!

YOU STUPID CLONES! GO GET HIM!
You know what you're doing, Uncle Grandpa?
Don't I always?
WE'RE DOOMED!
Ahem! CLONES! LISTEN TO ME!
Huh? Why didn't he flip the switch?
Who knows, man.
My clone brothers, look inside yourselves! My blood is *your* blood!
So please, find your inner Uncle Grandpa!
UG

Everything that is good and joyful and fun that is in me... is in YOU! FIND IT!
It's not working!
Find your inner Uncle Grandpa!
Amy! NO! COME BACK!
GRAAAWL!
Hurh?
NOOOOO!
RAAAARRRRR!
GLOMP

I love you, Uncle Grandpa.
Go-go-go- BZZZ- BZZZZZZ--
GOOD MOOOORNING!
Ha ha!
Everyone! Start hugging the clones! Make them laugh! Anything!
Aw man, do we have to? They smell weird.
GROWL!
Okay okay okay

Aw'right, guys! You're doing it!
Oh no, these clones are still evil!
UG
Quick! Make them laugh!
I can't just be put on the spot like that, I gotta-- oops!
WHOMP!
Ha ha haaaa! Man hurt, man funny!
Way to go, Uncle Grandpa!
Every-thing inside my body is now broken.
Uncle! Grandpa! Uncle! Grandpa!
We did it! We saved the day!

NO NO NO! What are you doing? This isn't part of my plan! Go back to being evil! NOW!
AGHHHHH
TRIP!
SPLUT
You fools!
C'mon! Turn back evil! You have a job to finish!
EEEEEEVIL!
SLAP SLAP SLAP SLAP SLAP SLAP SLAP
Heh heh! That tickle!

It's over, weird not-so-good version of me. Let's all just go home.
What do you say, buddy?
HA! It's not over until I say it's over!
Huh?
ZZZIP
Whoa un-cool, duuuuuuude!
Uncle Grandpa!
Ha ha HAAAAA!
Uhhh, what the heck just happened?
Nothing good, that's for sure.

Huh? Whazah?
Whoa! Where are we?
I think we are inside Nega-Uncle Grandpa's Nega-Belly Bag...but it's so... EMPTY!
I wonder...is this the artist's lame attempt to take it easy for a few pages?
Nooooo, surely not! He would never do that! WINK!
It's "empty" because unlike your Belly Bag, I keep mine neat, organized, and only keep what I need in here.
Whoa, you look all sooped up and junk!
Because in HERE, I am in control.
You're in MY world now! MY Nega-Uncle Grandpaland, if you will!
BOFF

THIS is a world of order! Of rules!
Blech. How boring!
Boring? BORING?
How is THIS for "boring" rules? I body slam you at a very fast speed--
WHOMP
Towards the street below--
And you go SPLAT.
SPLAT

HA! Finally! I can be at peace!
Oh man, that's gonna sting in the morning!
Wha...how... but...How did you survive that?
Well, I just thought it would be funnier if I bounced back from such a fall.
Heh, I even left an Uncle Grandpa shaped imprint on the ground! See? Funny!
Ha ha, good one, Uncle Grandpa!
But...but none of that makes any sense!
Exactly! That's the point!
I mean, how do you think I can do all this crazy noodle arm sort of stuff?
Okay, so I can't use physical attacks on you...

Maybe *psychological* attacks will do the trick!
Ha! Psychological? I don't even know the meaning of the word!
It's true. He really doesn't.
*MIND* games, you simpleton.
Again, I don't know the meaning.
Uh oh, I don't like where this is going!
Oh, hey guys! How'd you get in here?
Uuuhhh...
Look at this loser. *You've* been holding us back all these years!
Always dealing with your oddball and nonsensical adventures!
We'd all be better off if we had never met you!
GROWL!
Wh... what?
Don't listen to 'em, Uncle Grandpa!
But... you're my friends...
Are we really, though?

Oh geez oh geez oh geez...
Hey. Uncle Grandpa...
Huh? Are you the mean Belly Bag?
No, it's me, the one and only REAL Belly Bag.
Don't let this guy play these mind games with you!
C'mon, you know us better than that! We would NEVER say or think these mean things about you! We are your FRIENDS! We are here for you. Always.
Yeah You'r right
I think I get it, Nega-Uncle Grandpa.
What? No, this is impossible!
I know I'm not everyone's cup of tea. I'm the goofball.
The random weirdo. And that's okay.
But sometimes in this dark and serious world of ours, we need a little silliness. A little nonsense.
A little Uncle Grandpa.

But there's always a time and place for following the rules. For order. These are good things too.
There is a place in this world for **both** of us. In balance.
So what do you say? You look like you could use a good friend.
No. ***NEVER!*** I don't need YOU. I don't need ***FRIENDS.***
I DON'T NEED ANYONE!
Then I'm sorry.
Huh?
ZZZZZZZIP

No! NOOOOOOOO! You're not playing fair!
You goof ball! You scatterbrain! You zany-- AGGHHHH!
And that's the end of THAT!
ZZZZip
Wow, Uncle Grandpa! That was all so deep and zen and stuff!
Where did that all come from?
Huh? What?
Sorry, I zoned out there for a minute. What did I miss?
Whoa, what is that? Did you have burritos for lunch again, Belly Bag? We talked about that.
Oh no...
We trapped him and his Nega-Belly Bag inside of me while we are already inside HIS Nega-Belly Bag!
Dang it, I'm an Uncle Grandpa, not a doctor!
What does that all mean?
We just created a rift in the space-time continuum!
WE'RE GOING TO EXPLODE AND TAKE EVERYTHING IN A TEN MILE RADIUS WITH US!

Uhh...what's happening?
My guess, a fracture in time and space that will destroy us all. But that's just a guess.
Everyone RUN!

We're going to need a *miracle* to survive this!
SKREEEEEEEECH!
UG
How about a *TINY* Miracle?
*Tiny Miracle!*
I saw what was happening and quickly unbolted the RV from--
Yeah, okay. Now move over, we gotta get everyone out of here!
UG-RV
Move move *MOVE!* Everyone get your buns in here!
Can we *ALL* fit in there?
No fear, lady! It's pretty roomy on the inside!

Is that everyone?
Yeah... everyone but Uncle G and Belly Bag!
Should... should we wait for them?
No. That thing is about to explode! We gotta get everyone to safety. It's... what Uncle Grandpa would have wanted.
But... but...
Mreow!
Good-bye, Uncle Grandpa...

Well...I guess this is really the end, *huh?*
*Sniff.* Yeah...
You think the gang got everyone off the island and to safety?
*Oh* yeah, I'm sure of it. They're a good bunch. The ***BEST*** bunch!
If it's one thing I've learned, it's that ya always gotta believe in your friends.
*Aw,* that's pretty corny, Uncle Grandpa.
***Ha ha,*** yeah. But it's still true.
We had a good run though, right, Uncle Grandpa?
We sure did, Belly Bag. We sure did.

Good
morn--
BOOM
HOT
DOGS

Mr. Gus! Go back down! Maybe he... maybe...
No one...sniff... no one could have survived that.

He...he sacrificed himself for us.
All of us.
Thank you, Uncle Grandpa.
UG

SPLASH
SPLASH
Help! I can't swim!
I never bothered to earn that merit badge!
My excuse is that I'm an article of clothing!
UNCLE GRANDPA!
UG
You're... you're alive!
I won't be for much longer if you don't fish me out of here, guys!
Oh, HEY Belly Bag, you're okay too? Yeah! Oh, that's great!
After careful consideration, I don't think it was a good idea to open up a theme park.
Ha ha, you think?
How did you survive that?
I guess we just got thrown clean from the blast! Lucky us, I guess.

Okay, let's go home every-body!

So...what are we gonna do with all these Uncle Grandpa clones? There sure are a lot of them.
Hmm...
You know...I think I have just the thing!
SNAP!

A FEW WEEKS LATER...
CRASH!
Aw man, not again!
Yeah, we learned absolutely nothing.
RRRRUMMMMBL
What... what is that?
YAAAAAY! UNCLE GRANDPA!
CRASH
UG-1138

Uncle Grandpa?
Is he...?
Koff koff
GOOOOOOOOO'D MORNIIIIINNNG!
Huh?
Why does he look like that?
Broke vase? We fix!
We buy new vase!
No no no, that won't do at all!
Eep!

Your solution needs to be zanier and more fun and overly complicated! C'mon, Clone-1138, you totally got this!
Okie dokie!
Who's he talking to?
We now go to ancient lost city in Himalayas to find replacement!
Yeah, now you're cooking with fire!
Whoa, sweet!
We should break this vase more often!
Wha...?
Bye, Mom! We'll be home for dinner!
Here we go, kids!
UG
UNCLE GRANDPAAAAAAA!

Alright, you got it from here, UG-1138! Good job!
Thank yoooou!
I tell ya, Uncle Grandpa, this program is a huge success!
I know! Now I can sorta be everywhere at once and help *waaaaay* more kids!
And now I have all this free time on my hands!
Yo, maybe we can all take a vacation. I think we earned it!
Mrow.
Say, that's a great idea! I know just the place too!
There's this theme park I've been dying to go to!
FUN-LAND!
Groooooan! Uncle Grandpa!
RARW!
What? Was it something I said?
END!